Vehicles
On The Move

Motorcycles

Molly Aloian

❦ Crabtree Publishing Company

www.crabtreebooks.com

Created by Bobbie Kalman

Author
Molly Aloian

Editorial director
Kathy Middleton

Project editor
Paul Challen

Editors
Adrianna Morganelli
Crystal Sikkens

Proofreaders
Janine Belzak
Rachel Stuckey

Photo research
Melissa McClellan

Design
Melissa McClellan

Print coordinator
Katherine Berti

Production coordinator
Margaret Amy Salter

Prepress technicians
Margaret Amy Salter
Ken Wright

Consultant
Michael McFadden

Illustrations
All illustrations by Leif Peng

Photographs
Dreamstime.com: © Lforquer (title page); © David P. Smith (page 4); © Yury Maryunin (page 5); © Mylightscapes (page 6 bottom); © Jeff Cleveland (page 6 top); © Krzyssagit (page 7 bottom); © Juri Bizgajmer (pages 8–9); © Mlan61 (page 10); © Mark Atkins (page 12); © Shariff Che' Lah (pages 14–15); © Hupeng (page 16); © Linda Morland (page 18 bottom inset); © Radu Razvan Gheorghe (page 20); © Alvaro Ennes (page 21 top); © Sean Nel (pages 22–23); © Bstefanov (page 24); © Paolo Cipriani (page 25 top); © Asian (page 25 bottom); © Pg-images (page 26); © Crazy80frog (page 27); © Intst (page 28 top and bottom); © Margojh (page 30); © Mlan61 (page 31 bottom)
Public Domain: TTTNIS (page 21)
Shutterstock.com: cover; © Ben Heys (table of contents page); © Inc (page 7 top); © Iurii Davydov (page 11 top); © Losevsky Pavel (page 11 bottom); © Graham Prentice (page 13); © afaizal (page 15 top inset); © Dusan Dobes (page 17); © David Arts (pages 18–19); © Werner Stoffberg (page 22 inset); © Randy Miramontez (page 29 top and bottom); © ChipPix (page 31 top)

Library and Archives Canada Cataloguing in Publication

Aloian, Molly
    Motorcycles / Molly Aloian.

(Vehicles on the move)
Includes index.
Issued also in electronic format.
ISBN 978-0-7787-2730-9 (bound).--ISBN 978-0-7787-2737-8 (pbk.)

    1. Motorcycles--Juvenile literature. I. Title. II. Series:
Vehicles on the move

TL440.15.A46 2011   j629.227'5   C2011-900142-X

Library of Congress Cataloging-in-Publication Data

Aloian, Molly.
    Motorcycles / Molly Aloian.
        p. cm. -- (Vehicles on the move)
    Includes index.
    ISBN 978-0-7787-2730-9 (reinforced lib. bdg. : alk. paper) --
ISBN 978-0-7787-2737-8 (pbk. : alk. paper) -- ISBN 978-1-4271-9699-6
(electronic (PDF))
    1. Motorcycles--Juvenile literature. I. Title.
TL440.15.A46 2011
629.227'5--dc22
                                                    2010052349

Crabtree Publishing Company

www.crabtreebooks.com   1-800-387-7650

Printed in the U.S.A./022011/CJ20101228

Published in Canada
Crabtree Publishing
616 Welland Ave.
St. Catharines, ON
L2M 5V6

Published in the United States
Crabtree Publishing
PMB 59051
350 Fifth Avenue, 59th Floor
New York, New York 10118

Published in the United Kingdom
Crabtree Publishing
Maritime House
Basin Road North, Hove
BN41 1WR

Published in Australia
Crabtree Publishing
386 Mt. Alexander Rd.
Ascot Vale (Melbourne)
VIC 3032

Contents

Motoring!

A motorcycle is a vehicle. Vehicles are machines that move from place to place. Motorcycles have two wheels like a bicycle but are powered by a motor like a car. They are a lot of fun to ride because they are fast and move easily. You can often see motorcycles speeding along highways and other roads.

Motorcycling is a very popular way to tour the country. This rider has to lean the motorcycle to the side to make it turn.

Different motorcycles

There are different types of motorcycles. Many of them are fast and powerful! Some motorcycles are made to be driven on smooth racetracks and roads. Others are designed to climb steep mountain slopes or haul heavy loads. Motorcycles are also called motorbikes.

Some motorcycles are built to travel on trails and through the mud.

Open road

Motorcycles can go places that cars or trucks cannot go. Soldiers and police officers often ride on motorcycles because they are fast and agile. In busy cities, police on motorcycles can weave through cars in traffic jams and dart into narrow alleyways.

Motorcycles follow the same rules of the road as other vehicles.

Police officers on motorcycles can watch for vehicles that are driving over the speed limit.

City or country

In cities with very narrow streets, motorcycles are a fast and safe way to get around. In the country, some farmers ride on motorcycles called dirt bikes to round up cattle. In the United States, more than six million people have motorcycles.

Mud and dirt cannot stop an experienced rider on a dirt bike.

More than one rider can fit on a larger motorcycle.

Take a closer look

Motorcycles are made up of many parts. Each part does a different job. This motorcycle is a racing motorcycle. It is designed to go very fast.

gas tank

seat

taillight

exhaust and muffler

rear wheel

foot peg

engine

A motorcycle has an **engine**. The engine gives the motorcycle power. Power is what makes the motorcycle move.

mirror

wind screen

headlight

front wheel

Staying safe

A person who rides a motorcycle must wear special gear to stay safe. Riding a motorcycle can be dangerous if it is not done correctly. A motorcyclist should wear a **helmet**. A helmet protects the head. Many motorcyclists also wear leather gloves, boots, pants, and jackets to protect their bodies if they fall.

This rider is wearing a full-face helmet, which protects his head, face, and jaw.

Learning how

Motorcyclists must also learn how to steer, go forward, and stop on the motorcycle. You steer a motorcycle the same way you steer a bicycle, by turning the handlebars. Turning the throttle makes the motorcycle speed up. A motorcycle has a front and back brake. Pressing or squeezing the brakes slows the motorcycle down.

The front brake is found on the motorcycle's right handlebar.

Motorcycles have instruments just like a car—headlight beam, turn signals, horn, fuel gauge, and speedometer.

On the road

Road or street motorcycles are made to be driven on roads. One kind of road motorcycle is called a touring or cruising motorcycle. A **touring motorcycle** is good for long trips on highways. It may have a seat for a second rider behind the main seat.

Ride on

Touring motorcycles often have larger gasoline tanks than other motorcycles so the driver does not have to stop as often for gas during long rides. These motorcycles also have windshields to protect the riders from wind and weather during long trips.

A touring motorcycle often has big, comfortable seats.

Racing

Another kind of road motorcycle is called a racing motorcycle or sport motorcycle. **Racing motorcycles** are smaller and lighter than touring motorcycles and they are not as comfortable. But they are faster and more exciting to drive!

Fast and powerful

Racing motorcycles can travel more than 200 miles per hour (322 km/h). These motorcycles are light, but they have very powerful engines. They are good at accelerating, braking quickly, and turning tight corners.

Racing motorcycles have a streamlined shape that lets them cut through the air easily.

Harley-Davidson

The Harley-Davidson Motor Company is a well-known motorcycle manufacturer. It was founded in 1903 by William Harley, Arthur Davidson, Walter Davidson, and William Davidson. The company's headquarters are in Milwaukee, Wisconsin, in the United States.

Harley-Davidson motorcycles are easy to spot because of their unique design.

Police Work

"Harleys" are very popular road motorcycles. Harley-Davidson has also made thousands of police motorcycles. The first one was built in 1908. More than 3,000 police departments use Harley-Davidson motorcycles in the U.S. alone. Police departments in 45 other countries also ride Harley-Davidson motorcycles. These machines are known for their powerful engines and reliability.

Harley-Davidson motorcycles are very popular on many police forces.

Choppers

A motorcycle that has been changed or custom-made by the owner is called a **chopper**. Many people change their Harley-Davidson motorcycles into choppers. They paint them different colors, put on different rims and tires, and change the engines.

People who like to ride choppers often ride their customized motorcycles at special events.

Built from scratch

Some people build their own motorcycles from scratch. These choppers are very special because they can take a long time to build. Some of the most famous Harley-Davidson choppers were used in a movie called *Easy Rider*.

Scooters

Scooters are small, light motorcycles. They cannot go as fast as other motorcycles, but they use less fuel. They are cheaper to drive than regular motorcycles and cars, especially in cities where fuel is expensive. Some scooters, including the BMW C1, have roofs to keep riders dry in the rain!

Because of their size, scooters can get around crowded cities easily. They are also easy to park in tight spaces.

Fast and light

The Honda Silver Wing is one of the most powerful scooters around. It looks like a cruising motorcycle, but is still very light. It can reach a top speed of approximately 100 miles per hour (161 km/h).

The Vespa scooter was first produced in 1946. Vespas are one of the most popular models of scooter.

The Honda Silver Wing scooter is easier to drive than regular motorcycles.

Off-road

Off-road motorcycles are sometimes called dirt bikes. These medium-sized motorcycles are lightweight and strong. They have large wheels with knobby tires. They are good at traveling on dirt roads, through thick mud, and up steep hills.

Dirt bike riders can navigate on hilly, rough terrain in all types of weather.

Trail breaking

Some off-road motorcycles can go just about anywhere! They can climb up steep mountain slopes, plow through deep mud, and even pull heavy loads of equipment. In some countries, military forces even use these tough motorcycles instead of other army vehicles.

Crossing a river or stream is easy if your bike has enough power and the right tires!

23

Motocross

Motocross bikes are used for off-road motorcycle racing called motocross. During a motocross race, motorcyclists race around specially designed dirt tracks. The tracks have big hill jumps, flat sections, obstacles, and other features.

There is a wide range of age and skill divisions for motocross racers.

Watch this!

A motocross race can be very exciting to watch! Motocross bikes cannot go as fast as racing motorcycles. But motocross bikes are good at jumping and landing. They also have knobby tires to help them move through dirt.

Motocross helmets have goggles that fit firmly inside the helmet.

It takes a lot of training for a rider to be able to make difficult jumps and control a bike in the air.

Going the distance

An **Enduro** is a long-distance motorcycle race. There are different races for different kinds of motorcycles, but all of the races are very long. Some races can be over 5,000 miles (8,000 km) long and last one week or more!

Rocks and stones are no match for an experienced rider and a sturdy bike.

Tough stuff

The motorcycles used during Enduro races are similar to motocross bikes. These motorcycles have to be tough because the races usually take place over rough terrain such as the Australian Outback or the deserts of Africa.

Enduro riders have to be very fit to travel through the desert and other difficult terrain.

Stunt bikes

Some people perform dangerous stunts, or tricks, on motorcycles. They jump over rows of cars or ride through flames on their motorcycles. They also do wheelies. A wheelie is riding on just the back wheel of a motorcycle.

A wheelie is when the rider lifts the front wheel of the motorbike off the ground and rides only on the back wheel.

A stoppie is when the rider lifts the rear wheel of the motorcycle off the ground and rides only on the front wheel.

Acrobatic jumps

Another way to do tricks on a motorcycle is to ride it over a ramp, so that the motorcycle flies through the air. Riders can do all kinds of flips and spins, and sometimes push themselves up on the handlebars, or stand on them to make their jumps look really great!

Freestyle motocross is a sport where riders attempt to score points with jumps and stunts.

The ramps used for jumps are usually made out of metal.

Classic bikes

Motorcycles have been around for over 125 years, but they were not always the sleek racing machines that they are today. In 1885, a man named Gottlieb Daimler built the first vehicle called a motorcycle. It was an engine attached to a wooden bike.

The Excelsior Motorcycle company was one of the biggest motorcycle makers of the 1910s and '20s. This bike is from 1911.

Pedal power

Early motorcycles were called "boneshakers" because riders shook as they traveled over rough country roads. Some of these early motorcycles had pedals so the riders could help power the motorcycle.

Passenger sidecars were very popular on early motorcycles.

Riders of early bikes were probably not as comfortable on their motorcycles as they are today, but their vehicles still helped them travel on roads and trails.

Words to know and Index

chopper
pages 18–19

helmet
pages 10, 25

motocross bikes
pages 24, 25, 27, 29

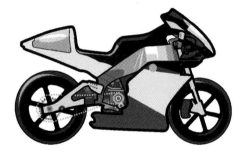

racing motorcycle
pages 8, 9, 14, 15, 25, 30

touring motorcycle
pages 12–13

scooter
pages 20–21

Other index words